22x 5/10 *2/13 (04-10)

MM ✓

Land and Water

The Nile River

by Mike Graf

Consultant:
Robert M. Hordon, Ph.D., P.H.
Department of Geography
Rutgers University
Piscataway, New Jersey

Capstone
press

Mankato, Minnesota

Fact Finders is published by Capstone Press
151 Good Counsel Drive, P.O. Box 669, Mankato, Minnesota 56002
www.capstonepress.com

Library of Congress Cataloging-in-Publication Data
Graf, Mike.
   The Nile river / by Mike Graf.
   p. cm.—(Fact finders. Land and water)
   Includes bibliographical references and index.
   Contents: The Nile River—The Nile's path—The Nile's history—The Nile's
people—Using the Nile—The Nile today.
   ISBN 0-7368-2484-7 (hardcover)
   1. Nile River—Juvenile literature. [1. Nile River.] I. Title. II. Series.
DT117 .G73 2004
962—dc22   2003016510

Editorial Credits

Erika L. Shores, editor; Juliette Peters, series designer; Linda Clavel, book designer and
   illustrator; Alta Schaffer, photo researcher; Eric Kudalis, product planning editor

Photo Credits

Blaine Harrington III, 16–17, 24–25
Corbis/Lloyd Cluff, 20–21
Index Stock Imagery/David Bell, cover
Joe McDonald/Tom Stack & Associates, 10
Mary & Lloyd McCarthy/Root Resources, 22–23
Michele Burgess, 1, 11
North Wind Picture Archives, 4–5, 14, 15
TRIP/H. Rogers, 7, 12–13, 18, 19, 27

Artistic Effects

Image Ideas Inc.

1 2 3 4 5 6 09 08 07 06 05 04

Table of Contents

Chapter 1

The Nile River

About 5,000 years ago, Egyptians began to plant crops near a great river flowing through their land. Crops grew well in the rich, dark soil. Each year, the the river overflowed its banks, leaving behind more **fertile** soil. Egyptians called this river *Iteru*. Today, it is called the Nile.

The Nile today is different from the river the **ancient** Egyptians knew. People have built **dams** along the river. The dams have changed the way people use the river. But the river is still important to the millions of people who live along it.

Ancient Egyptians built the Great Pyramids near the Nile. They buried their leaders in these tombs.

The River

The Nile is the longest river in the world. It flows north 4,160 miles (6,695 kilometers). It starts in the small African country of Burundi and flows into the Mediterranean Sea.

The Nile gets its name from the Greek word *nelios*. It means river valley. The Nile's water is used to water crops and to make electricity. It is also home to many wild animals such as crocodiles and hippopotamuses.

FACT!

The Nile is considered the giver of life to all of Egypt. It was once believed that if you drink from the Nile, you will come back to live again in another life.

Millions of people live in
the Nile River valley.

Chapter 2

The Nile's Path

Two rivers join to make the Nile River. The Luvironza River flows out of Burundi into Lake Nyanza. This lake is also called Lake Victoria. There, the river leaves the lake and becomes the White Nile. In northern Ethiopia, the Blue Nile begins near Lake Tana. The Blue Nile flows over Tisisat Falls and passes through mountains. In Sudan, the White Nile and Blue Nile meet. They form the Nile River.

The River Valley

From Sudan, the Nile flows north. It passes through Egypt on its way to the Mediterranean Sea. At the north end is the Nile **Delta**. At the delta, the Nile breaks into two branches. The Rosetta flows west. The Damietta flows east.

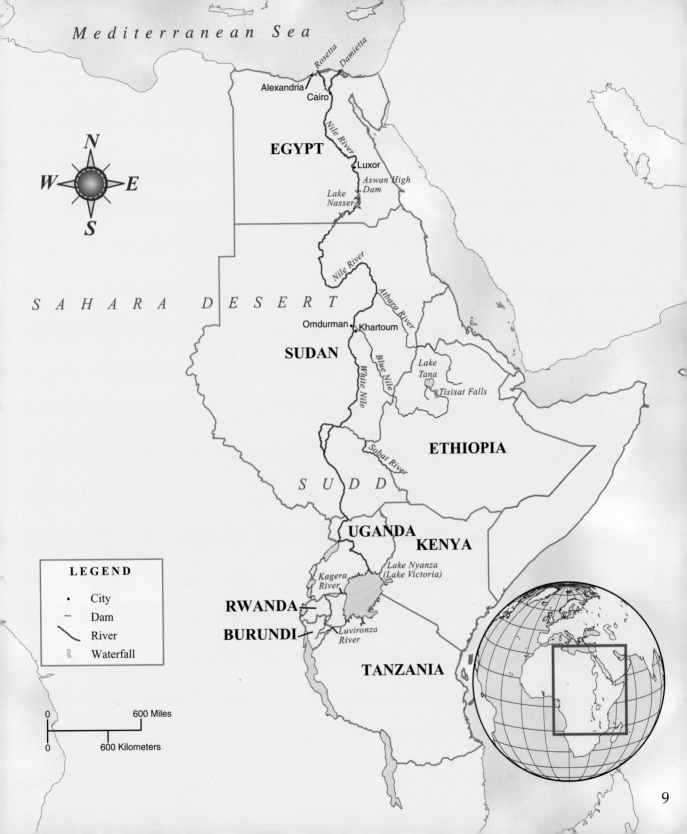

Mediterranean Sea

Rosetta *Damietta*

Alexandria
Cairo

EGYPT

Nile River

Luxor

Aswan High Dam

Lake Nasser

Nile River

S A H A R A   D E S E R T

Atbara River

Omdurman • Khartoum

SUDAN

Blue Nile

Lake Tana

Tisisat Falls

White Nile

ETHIOPIA

Sobat River

S U D D

UGANDA

KENYA

Lake Nyanza (Lake Victoria)

Kagera River

RWANDA

BURUNDI

Luvironza River

TANZANIA

N
W E
S

LEGEND
• City
– Dam
— River
| Waterfall

0 ———— 600 Miles
0 ———— 600 Kilometers

9

Swamps

The White Nile flows through an area in Sudan called the Sudd. This area is the world's largest swamp. Crocodiles, elephants, and giraffes are some of the animals that live here.

The delta is an area of shallow lakes and swamps. It is 120 miles (190 kilometers) wide. Farmers grow wheat, cotton, and rice in the delta's rich soil.

The Nile crocodile lives in swamps near the Nile.

Climate

The Nile River **basin** has two **climates**. The south has heavy rainfall. The north is dry. Mountains in the south have high temperatures of about 68 degrees Fahrenheit (20 degrees Celsius). The northern desert receives little or no rain. Temperatures there can reach 120 degrees Fahrenheit (49 degrees Celsius).

▲ Farmers need water from the Nile to grow their crops.

The Sahara Desert

Most of the Nile flows through the eastern part of the Sahara Desert. The Sahara Desert is the world's largest desert. People living there need the Nile River to bring water to their crops.

F A C T !

The Sahara Desert covers almost one-third of Africa.

11

Chapter 3

The Nile's History

People have lived in the Nile River valley for thousands of years. About 10,000 years ago, people began to fish, hunt, and gather berries and seeds along the river. At that time, the area was full of swamps and grasses. Many wild animals lived near the river.

Traveling on the Nile

Ancient Egyptians made boats for traveling on the Nile. They tied reeds together to make boats and paddles.

To travel north, boats floated with the river **current**. Sails were used to travel south using the wind. Egyptians were some of the first people to use sails.

Paintings made by ancient Egyptians show what life was like on the Nile.

Watering Crops

Ancient Egyptians began to **irrigate** crops in 5500 B.C. They carried bags of water from the Nile to their crops. Around 2500 B.C., people built dams on the Nile. From the dams, they dug **canals** to bring water to their crops.

Around 1550 B.C., the Egyptians invented the *shaduf*. It is an irrigation tool made by attaching a bucket to a pole. People dipped the bucket into the water, lifted it, and turned it. This method took water from the river and put it into a canal. Some Egyptian farmers still use the *shaduf* today.

Egyptians used a *shaduf* to bring water from the Nile to their crops.

Exploring the Nile

In 1788, British scientist Joseph Banks founded the African Association. This group wanted to explore Africa. The group's first trips focused on the Sahara Desert and the Nile River. The group wanted to find the source of the Nile.

In 1858, British army officer John Hanning Speke explored the Nile. He believed he had found the White Nile's main water source at Lake Nyanza. In 1875, Henry Morton Stanley traveled to Lake Nyanza. His trip proved that Speke was right.

▲ John Hanning Speke discovered the source of the White Nile at Lake Nyanza.

FACT!

Speke died the day before he was to defend his claim of finding the source of the White Nile. He accidentally shot himself while hunting.

Chapter 4

The Nile's People

The Nile River flows through eight countries in Africa. Many people in these countries build their homes near the river. They also hunt and fish in the river. Some people live in small villages. Other people live in large cities on the Nile.

Cities on the Nile

Cairo, Egypt, is Africa's largest city. It is in the Nile Delta. Nearly 10 million people live in and around Cairo. Today, much of the delta's good farming land has homes and businesses built on it. Cairo's government wants to use the delta to grow more crops.

Cairo, Egypt, is the largest city on the Nile River.

The government has asked some people from Cairo to move. The land will be used for farmland. New towns have formed on the edge of the Nile Delta.

Three cities are on the Nile's banks where the White and Blue Niles meet. The cities are Khartoum, Khartoum North, and Omdurman. The cities are Sudan's center for government, **industry**, and trade.

Khartoum, Sudan, is where the White and Blue Niles meet.

▲ Some villagers
come to the
banks of the
Nile to wash
their clothing.

Village Life on the Nile

Small villages line the Nile. People in these villages grow crops along the river. They also fish for catfish and perch.

People use the Nile's water for other things besides food. Many people living along the Nile wash their clothes in the river. They also bathe animals, such as camels and donkeys, in the Nile.

Chapter 5

Using the Nile

Water is the most important resource in the Sahara Desert. Some countries in the area have said they are willing to fight wars over water. Egypt and Sudan have struggled for 2,000 years over who has rights to the Nile's water.

Aswan High Dam

In the 1960s, Egypt, along with help from the former Soviet Union, began to build the Aswan High Dam. It was completed in 1970. The dam created Lake Nasser. Lake Nasser is the second-largest human-made lake in the world.

The Aswan High Dam is 364 feet (111 meters) high and about 2 miles (3 kilometers) long.

Lake Nasser's water has many uses. It is used to irrigate farms. People also fish in the lake. Water flowing through the Aswan High Dam makes electricity for Egyptians.

Harming the Soil

Farmers downstream from the Aswan High Dam are suffering. Before the dam was built, the Nile flooded almost every year. When it did, it left fertile soil along its banks.

Now, the dam has stopped the flooding. Farmers have to use **fertilizers** to grow their crops. Fertilizers are costly and they do not make the soil as rich as before.

The dam also causes the Nile to flow more slowly. The slow flow allows salt water from the Mediterranean Sea to flow upriver. Salt water ruins soil. It also gets into wetlands and harms animals and their homes.

Farmers along the Nile use fertilizers to help their crops grow.

Chapter 6

The Nile Today

Today, the Nile River continues to be the giver of life in northeast Africa. People living in the eastern Sahara Desert and other areas near the river could not live without the river.

Farms are all along the Nile River. Farmers transport crops on the Nile. Water from the Nile is also used to irrigate crops. Irrigation makes it possible to grow crops in the desert.

Fishing is popular on the Nile. For some people, fishing is their main source of income. They catch perch and catfish to sell at markets.

People living along the Nile travel by boat from place to place.

Tourism

Many people come to Egypt to visit the Nile. Every day, cruise ships travel up and down the river. Traditional sailboats called *feluccas* also travel on the Nile. These boats drop off people at popular tourist sites.

Tourists visit Giza near Cairo. This city is home to the three Great Pyramids. People also can see the Great Sphinx in Giza.

The Nile's Future

As the population in the Nile River valley grows, the demand for the river's water increases. Some people want to build more canals to bring the Nile's water to even more land. As long as it flows to the sea, people will continue to use and change the Nile River.

Visitors to the Nile River can sail on *feluccas*.

Fast Facts

Sources: The White Nile's source is the Luvironza River in Burundi. The Blue Nile's source is Lake Tana in Ethiopia.

Outlet: Mediterranean Sea

Name: Nile comes from the word *nelios*, which means river valley.

Major tributaries: Atbara River, Sobat River, Kagera River

Explorers: Joseph Banks, John Hanning Speke, Henry Morton Stanley

Major industries: farming, tourism, fishing

Major cities: Cairo, Egypt; Khartoum, Sudan; Alexandria, Egypt; Luxor, Egypt

Hands On: Make a Felucca

Thousands of years ago, ancient Egyptians used boats and sails to travel on the Nile River. Today, people still use sailboats to travel on the Nile. These sailboats are called *feluccas*. Try this activity to make your own sailboat.

What You Need

adult helper
small paper milk carton
scissors
drinking straw
ruler
tape
paper
sink or dishpan filled with water

What You Do

1. Ask an adult to cut the milk carton in half lengthwise. The carton will be the boat.
2. Use the scissors to cut two 1-inch (2.5-centimeter) slits across from each other in the bottom of the straw.
3. Now, fold out the cut ends of the straw and tape them flat to the bottom of the carton.
4. Use the scissors to cut a triangle from the piece of paper. Tape the longest side of the triangle to the straw. The straw and triangle make the boat's sail.
5. Place your *felucca* in the sink or dishpan. Blow on the boat's sail. Does your *felucca* move?

Glossary

ancient (AYN-shunt)—very old

basin (BAY-suhn)—an area of land around a river from which water drains into the river

canal (kuh-NAL)—a channel dug across land which water can flow through

climate (KLEYE-mit)—the usual weather that occurs in a place

current (KUR-uhnt)—the fastest-flowing part of a river or stream

dam (DAM)—a strong wall built across a stream or river to hold water back

delta (DEL-tuh)—the area where a river meets the sea; the Nile River splits into many smaller branches to form a delta.

fertile (FUR-tuhl)—good for growing crops

fertilizer (FUR-tuh-lize-ur)—a substance added to soil to make crops grow better

industry (IN-duh-stree)—businesses that make products or provide services

irrigate (IHR-uh-gate)—to supply dry land with water through ditches, pipes, or streams

Internet Sites

FactHound offers a safe, fun way to find Internet sites related to this book. All of the sites on FactHound have been researched by our staff.

Here's how:
1. Visit *www.facthound.com*
2. Type in this special code **0736824847** for age-appropriate sites. Or enter a search word related to this book for a more general search.
3. Click on the **Fetch It** button.

FactHound will fetch the best sites for you!

Read More

Bowden, Rob. *The Nile.* A River Journey. Austin, Texas: Raintree Steck-Vaughn, 2004.

Cumming, David. *The Nile.* Great Rivers of the World. Milwaukee: World Almanac Library, 2003.

Johnson, Darv. *The Longest River.* Extreme Places. San Diego: KidHaven Press, 2003.

Index